CREATIVE BOTTLE CUTTING

ART AND FUNCTIONAL PROJECTS FROM OLD BOTTLES

B. KAY FRASER

CROWN PUBLISHERS, INC. · NEW YORK

Inquiries should
be addressed to Crown Publishers, Inc.,
419 Park Avenue South, New York, N.Y. 10016

Library of Congress Catalog Card Number: 72-89411
ISBN: 0-517-501139
ISBN: 0-517-502143
Printed in the United States of America
Published simultaneously in Canada by
General Publishing Company Limited

Contents

Chapter 1

Turn Trash to Treasure!

The exciting new hobby of bottle cutting is fast becoming one of the most popular crafts of creative people. Here's why: Bottle artists can solve litter problems, create unique personalized gifts, earn extra income, and fill their households with glasses, bowls, vases, lamps, wind chimes, ashtrays, and much, much more.

Plus, bottle cutting requires little time, less talent, and no money other than the original investment in a bottle cutting kit. All one needs is a bit of imagination and a lot of trash!

That's right...trash is the indispensable ingredient of successful bottle cutting. More specifically, used bottles and jugs that are normally discarded are required. With that bit of imagination and a bottle cutter, you can turn ketchup bottles into elegant vases; gallon jugs into pet food dishes; beer bottles into wind chimes; Tabasco bottles into earrings; wine jugs into bowls; pop bottles into tumblers; cooking oil jars into canisters.

Thus, when you turn trash to treasure, you not only gain a fascinating new hobby, but you help to solve an ecological problem: litter. Each bottle you use instead of throwing it away aids in making a better environment.

Ecology? Environment? . . . These are fairly modern terms to use when discussing a craft. But bottle cutting is a very contemporary craft. Although people have been trying to cut bottles for years with varying degrees of failure and frustration, it has been only in the past few years that bottles could be cut with repeated success.

Indeed, the hobby of bottle cutting didn't really gain momentum until the late 1960s when Floyd Fleming of Seattle, Washington, patented his bottle and jug cutter. With his invention, folks could scribe a line around the outside of a bottle; then tap this line from the inside of the bottle to complete the break. The bottle and jug cutter was as easy to operate as a can opener!

Since then other manufacturers have produced bottle cutters similar to Mr. Fleming's. Some have invented entirely different methods, such as scribing the bottle by rotating it in a box; then completing the break by heating with candle flame or electricity. And one manufacturer even offers a kit that cuts bottles in one step with an electrically charged wire.

The availability of these bottle cutting kits as well as the opportunity to create useful items from discarded bottles soon caused this new hobby to surge in popularity.

The number of bottle artists continues to swell as people discover that the hobby is not only practical and easy, but it's fun! All ages can express their creativity by cutting and assembling bottles as their imagination dictates. Persons from all walks of life can relax and forget everyday worries when concentrating on bottle art. And everybody can afford this hobby, for we all have trash that can be turned to treasure.

So let's begin the fun of creative bottle cutting!

Chapter 2

Gather Materials

All that's needed to turn trash to treasure is a bottle cutting kit, empty bottles, and a few accessories for decoration and safety. It is entirely possible to begin this lifetime hobby for less than a ten-dollar investment.

Bottle Cutting Kits

Bottles can be cut with a plain glass cutter from the hardware store. Although glass cutters work well on plain sheet glass where you can use a ruler or straight edge for a guide, it is difficult to cut a round bottle with a glass cutter because there is no circular guide. Plus, it is difficult to make an even line because too much pressure is required to scribe the glass.

Another way to cut a bottle, often used in the past, is to tie a string dipped in kerosene around it. Ignite the string, then submerge the bottle in cold water. The changes in temperature, which make the glass expand and contract, should cause the bottle to fracture along the string line. Unfortunately, it is nearly impossible to tie a string so it makes an even fracture line. So the bottle can crack above or below the string line—or send cracks shooting off in different directions!

Thus, in order to cut bottles with repeated success, you should invest in a bottle cutting kit. Such kits are specifically designed to cut round bottles accurately and to leave as smooth a cut edge as possible.

Most kits cut bottles in a two-part process. First, a thin line is scribed on the outside of the bottle exactly where it should break. Then the fracture is completed by either tapping the scribed line gently or by alternating temperatures to crack the glass molecules.

There are three basic types of bottle cutting kits on the market. All are very easy for a beginner to use and range in price from about seven dollars up to forty dollars. Price, however, is no indication of superiority. Rather, you should select a kit on the basis of which method you prefer.

Scribe-and-tap method. For example, the most common and least expensive type of bottle cutting kit features a cutting wheel and a tapper. The cutting wheel is attached to a vertical frame that fits in the neck of the bottle. The neck thus serves as a pivot point to guide the wheel in a straight line around the bottle . . . like a compass. After the wheel has scribed a line around the outside, the tapper is inserted inside the bottle. The tapper is then gently hammered parellel to the scribed line until the break is completed.

The scribe-and-tap method is most similar to that used by professional glass cutters. It is an extremely versatile kit that enables bottle artists to cut nearly any size bottle or jug; and the cutting wheel may be removed from the frame to create freehand bottle art. Some kits come unassembled but are easily put together in five minutes. The bottle itself may be cut in less than one minute with this method.

The scribe-and-tap method cuts a bottle in less than a minute with a cutting wheel and tapper.

Scribe-and-heat method. Another fun and popular way to cut bottles is with the scribe-and-heat method. Instead of scribing the bottle with a cutting wheel attached to a vertical frame, the bottle is scribed by a wheel attached to a horizontal box or cradle. In other words, the bottle is laid on its side in the "cradle," and rotated against the cutting wheel. Rather than using the neck of the bottle to maintain a straight scribe, this method relies upon a plate at the base of the bottle to keep it in place.

The fracture is also completed in a different manner. Instead of tapping against the scribed line, the bottle artist uses heat to finish the cut. Heat may be applied manually or electrically.

With a manual kit, you heat the bottle by holding the scribed line over a candle's flame. Then rub an ice cube around the scribe to immediately cool the bottle. The change in temperature causes the glass molecules to crack along the scribed line.

With an electric kit, you heat the bottle by placing a thin wire around the scribed line. The wire is then charged with electricity, which heats the bottle until it cracks. The bottle may then fall apart by itself or you may need to give it a slight tap with a table knife or screwdriver handle.

Whether you prefer a manual or electric kit, the scribe-and-heat method is extremely easy and is especially suitable for beginners and youngsters.

With the scribe-and-heat method, bottles are laid in a "cradle" and rotated against a cutting wheel. (Photo courtesy Ephrem's Olde Time Bottle Cutter Kit manufactured by Stylecraft of Baltimore.)

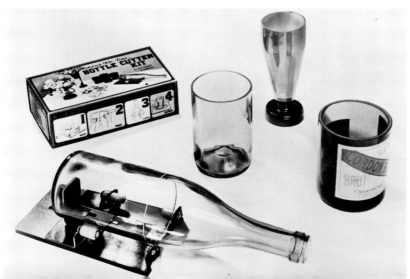

A safe, easy way to complete a fracture is to heat the scribed line with an electric wire.

Wire-cutting method. The third method of cutting bottles varies widely from the first two methods in that it requires only one step. A wire loop is fastened around the bottle and is then heated with electricity. As the heat penetrates the glass, the molecules will expand until the glass fractures. The process may take from about twenty seconds for no-deposit beer bottles up to two or three minutes for thick champagne bottles. The bottle may "pop" apart by itself, or it may be touched to a cool damp cloth to complete the fracture.

Although the wire-cutting method sounds very simple, it requires extreme care on the part of the bottle artist. The bottle should be marked beforehand with a felt-tip pen so you'll know exactly where to place the wire. The wire should be rotated so that the entire circumference of the bottle is heated evenly. With care, however, the wire-cutting method produces an extremely smooth cut and may be used on all shapes and sizes of bottles, both round and square.

The wire-cutting method requires one careful step to cut bottles.

Again, all bottle cutting kits work equally well. Which kit you select is simply a matter of personal choice. Some bottle artists use all three methods, depending upon what type of bottle they are cutting. And the methods are interchangeable. For example, you may scribe the bottle in the horizontal cradle; then complete the fracture with a tapper. Or, you may scribe the bottle with the cutting wheel on a vertical frame, then complete the break with an electric wire.

Most of the bottle kits mentioned can be found in hobby stores, discount centers, syndicate stores, mail order catalogs, and so on. If such stores are not near your home, you may order bottle cutting kits by writing to the following addresses:

Scribe-and-tap method
    Ila Mae Robinson
    Distributor, Fleming Bottle & Jug Cutter
    Route 1, Box 663
    Florence, Oregon 97439
    ($8.95 postpaid)

    Miracle Bottle Cutter
    Yorkshire House
    P.O. Box 280, Dept. KF
    Canby, Oregon 97013
    ($7.50 postpaid)

    Open End Glassmaker
    Open End, Inc.
    Box 471,
    Marblehead, Massachusetts 09145
    ($8.95 postpaid)

Scribe-and-heat method
    Ephrem's Olde Time Bottle Cutter Kit (manual)
    Stylecraft of Baltimore
    1800 Johnson Street
    Baltimore, Maryland 21230
    ($10.95 postpaid)

    Bottle Cutter Kit (electric)
        available at any of American Handicrafts' 210 stores across the
        nation for $15.95; for address of store nearest you, write to:
    American Handicrafts Company
    Central Warehouse
    1920 Eighth Avenue
    Fort Worth, Texas 76110

Wire-cutting method
    Electric Bottle Kutter
    Cannon Crafts Creations
    20254 Saticoy Street
    Canoga Park, California 91306
    ($31.95 plus $3 shipping charge for standard model,
      $39.95 plus $3 shipping charge for deluxe model)

Bottles, Bottles, Bottles

It's true . . . the best things in life are free! For the most important material this hobby requires costs absolutely nothing. Empty bottles are as close as your trash can.

Simply save all discarded bottles, such as those that once contained ketchup, cooking oil, vinegar, soy sauce, fruit juice, baby food, beer, wine, pop.

When you shop, select foods and beverages that are bottled in interesting containers. For example, if you buy 7-Up in return bottles instead of cans, you'll have the material for a set of "mod" tumblers. If you buy vinegar in gallon jugs instead of quarts, you'll soon have the material for a set of canisters. As a shopping guide, thumb through the following chapters to see what kind of bottles may be converted into "treasures."

Perhaps your family doesn't consume a product that is contained in bottles you desire. That's no problem. Simply spread the word among friends and relatives that you'll appreciate their cast-off bottles, and you'll have a roomful of material! Restaurant owners will gladly oblige with empty wine bottles and syrup jugs. Most folks are aware of today's litter problem and will gladly help you make use of "waste" materials.

Save all bottles that come your way. An old ketchup bottle may not look promising today; but tomorrow it may be exactly what you need to create a sudden inspiration. Even if you have a surplus of, say, a particular brand of beer bottles, keep extras on hand. When you cut these bottles into matching glasses or candle holders, not every cut will be perfect. So the extras may be necessary to complete a set.

Obviously you'll need a place to store all the empty bottles you collect. Most bottle cutting enthusiasts stash their bottles in empty cardboard boxes (free from the grocery store), then put the boxes in out-of-the-way places . . . such as garages, storage rooms, broom closets, even under the bed!

Today's trash can be cut into tomorrow's treasure.

Decorating Accessories

Although many bottle creations do not require any decoration, it is fun to add a dab of paint, a decal, a bit of gold braid, or such. In fact, hobby and variety stores are beginning to stock more and more items of interest to bottle artists.

For example, glass paints are a favorite decorating accessory. Such products as Cryst-L-Craze and Glas Stain will color plain bottles, creating beautiful lamps, candy dishes, Christmas decorations, wind chimes, and much more.

Another popular paint product is ball-point paint tubes; the paint may be waterproofed by baking. Ball-point paint tubes are often used for embroidery and thus may be found in the needlework section of syndicate and variety stores. With these tubes, you can copy designs and write personalized messages on bottles.

Many bottle artists also use glitter, yarn, buttons, marbles, tiny figures, and so forth to add glamour to cut bottles. Simple decals from the dime store can turn an ordinary bottle into an eye-catching creation. And even metallike designs can be added to glass with Liquid Lead or MagiCraft Craft Lead (also available in gold, silver, and steel).

With such a wide choice of decorating accessories, you can make your bottle treasures as fancy as you desire.

If, however, you prefer less ornate bottle art, perhaps the only decorating accessory you will need is a strong adhesive or epoxy that will enable you to bond bottle parts into creative shapes.

Adhesives and other decorating accessories will be discussed with instructional information in later chapters. In the meantime, keep your eyes open for decorative tidbits that can give your bottle art that "special touch."

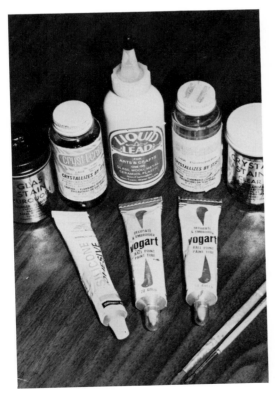

Many fun and easy decorating accessories for bottles are now on the market.

Safety Accessories

Cutting a bottle is no more hazardous than operating a can opener. However, certain precautions should be observed to protect you and your household from flying glass fragments.

First, always cut bottles in a well-lit area on a sturdy table- or countertop. Protect the work with layers of old newspaper. All grit will fall on the newspaper, which may be immediately discarded. Newspapers also protect tables from scratchy bottle edges. Keep a wastebasket handy to throw away any unwanted bottle parts or badly cut bottles.

Secondly, if you use heat—such as an electric wire or candle—to fracture a bottle, remove the bottle cap. Otherwise, the heat cannot escape and the bottle may explode.

Finally, after a bottle has been cut, do not rub your finger around the cut edge. The edge may look smooth, but it is still sharp enough to slice you until it is sanded, as explained in chapter 4.

By using such "commonsense" safety precautions, safety accessories may not be needed. Other safety pointers include: Keep fingers out of the cutter's way. Don't touch heated electric wires until they cool. Never put your eyes close to the bottle during scribing or fracturing.

For close-up work or processes where glass may fly more than usual, however, safety accessories are recommended. For example, safety goggles will protect your eyes from flying glass when drilling a hole in a bottle. A pair of gloves will save fingers from glass splinters when breaking glass with pliers, such as in making a chain of bottle rings.

In sum, then, bottle cutting is a safe hobby as long as you use common sense—or gloves and goggles!

Chapter 3

Ready, Set...Cut

Within fifteen minutes, many beginning bottle artists are able to create unique and useful items. They quickly discover the gentle pressure necessary for a successful scribe. And they agilely tap, heat, or alternate temperatures until the bottle is fractured with a smooth, even edge.

Other bottle artists are not so lucky. Their first bottles break unevenly, fracture in several directions, or—worse yet—won't break at all. If this should happen to you, don't give up! Even experienced bottle artists find that one out of three bottles may not break to their satisfaction.

With patience and practice, however, anyone can easily learn to cut bottles with a bottle cutting kit. When mistakes do occur, it is usually because the bottle itself is faulty; the bottle was scribed incorrectly; or the fracture was made too hastily.

Let's explore each of these reasons for failure so they will seldom happen to you!

Select a Bottle

No two bottles are alike. Even bottles made by the same manufacturer will vary. For example, one bottle may have thinner glass than the other. To complicate the matter further, a particular bottle may vary in thickness from one side to the other.

The difference in the thickness of the glass can cause bad separations. For example, when fracturing a bottle with alternating temperatures, the thinner part will readily break; but the thicker part may not break at all. (By repeating the heat-and-cool process several times, however, the thicker part will usually separate.) Or, say you are tapping a bottle to complete the fracture. A hearty tap will fracture the thicker part; but on thinner parts a tap of the same pressure may break the bottle or cause the fracture to sprout off in a different direction. (This problem is remedied by always starting to tap with gentle pressure.)

To determine if a bottle varies greatly in thickness and thinness lay it on a level table. When it stops rolling, the lighter weight thin glass will be up. Mark that side with a felt-tip pen. You'll then know which side of the bottle may cause problems during fracturing and can tap or alternate temperatures accordingly.

In addition to differing thickness of the glass, the shape of the bottle may cause problems. Some bottles won't "fit" your bottle cutter without adjustments. Wide-mouthed jars, for instance, require an improvised "pivot point" with the scribe-and-tap method. Very large jugs or tiny bottles will not fit into the cradle of the scribe-and-heat method without adjusting the cutting wheel. Square bottles can only be cut freehand or with the wire-cutting method. And no method works satisfactorily on bottles with dimensional designs, such as beverage bottles with lions or grapes molded in the glass. (But you can cut above or below such designs.)

Eventually you will want to experiment with "problem" bottles. To begin, however, *select perfectly round bottles that vary little in thickness and thinness.* No-deposit beer bottles are excellent for beginners and may be used as glasses and decorations.

If you prefer wine bottles, remember this general rule: the better the wine, the better the bottle. The thickness of the glass is more uniform; the color is often deeper; and mold seams are more even.

More important than the thickness of the glass or the shape of the bottle, however, is its cleanliness. Scribing over dirt, grease, or labels will not only cause a bad break, but it could dull your bottle cutter.

The easiest way to clean bottles is to let them soak in hot soapy water. In about twenty minutes, labels should slip off. Scour any remaining glue from the label, rinse, and let air dry. Or, you may dry the bottle with a lintless cloth. (Terry cloth dish towels leave fuzz on the bottle.)

Occasionally you'll encounter very stubborn labels that won't soak off, especially American wine and liquor labels. These may be peeled or scraped under hot running water. Or, fill the bottle with near-boiling water and place it upright in a pan of near-boiling water. The heat from the water will loosen the glue both inside and out so that the label can be gently removed from the bottle.

If you do not wish to remove the label, clean the rest of the bottle and cut either above or below the label.

Basic Bottle Cutting

Before scribing a bottle, first carefully read instructions in your bottle cutting kit. Granted, this advice sounds elementary. But you'd be amazed how many beginners meet with failure simply because they didn't follow the manufacturer's directions!

With the exception of the wire-cutting method, all bottle cutting kits rely upon three basic, easy steps:

1. Align the cutter at right angles to the bottle.
2. Scribe a hairline around the bottle.
3. Complete the fracture by tapping, alternating temperatures, or heating with an electric wire.

Step 1 is simple yet very important. The cutting wheel should rest against the bottle so that the cutter is perfectly straight. *If the cutting wheel is at right angles to the surface, it will produce a clean hairline cut.* If, however, the cutting wheel hits the glass at a slant, it will produce a rough frothy line that will not fracture evenly.

It's very easy to align the cutter at right angles. If you are using the scribe-and-heat method, place the bottle in the cradle. The cradle has a base plate that serves as a support and guide. Move this base plate forward or backward until the bottle fits snugly against it and the cutting wheel hits the bottle where you want to scribe. If you have selected a round bottle of normal size, the cutting wheel should then be at right angles.

With a scribe-and-tap kit, you will adjust the vertical frame that holds the cutter rather than adjust the base of a horizontal cradle. Place the cork (or pivot cone) in the neck of the bottle. Then loosen the wing nuts and readjust the frame until the vertical bar *is* vertical (align to the seam on the bottle, a doorframe, window frame) and the cutter is at a 90° angle to the bottle. When in place, tighten the wing nuts. Vertical frames also have a lower bar opposite the cutter that may be tightened against the bottle to further stabilize the cutter.

With a bit of practice, you will be able to align the bottle and cutting wheel correctly in a matter of seconds.

The cutting wheel should hit the bottle at right angles, never at a slant.

To make a perfect hairline cut, scribe the bottle with gentle, uniform pressure.

Step 2 is the fun step, scribing the bottle. Different manufacturers refer to this step as scribing, scoring, or etching. All terms are correct, for you will now create a hairline cut around the bottle.

To do this, merely rotate the bottle against the cutting wheel. With the scribe-and-tap method, you'll hold the vertical frame in place with one hand and turn the bottle against the cutter with your other hand. With the scribe-and-heat method, you may use one or both hands to rotate the bottle against the cutting wheel affixed to the cradle.

No matter which kit you're using, you'll create a perfect scribe if you *use gentle pressure and rotate the bottle in a continuous motion.*

The most common mistake of beginners is to force the bottle against the cutter, trying to make as deep an etch as possible. This is wrong. Too much pressure will make frothy cuts that may break unevenly . . . or may not break at all. You do not want to cut clear through the bottle (the fracture will be completed during Step 3.) You merely want to etch a barely visible line—thin as a human hair—on the outside of the bottle.

Naturally, this hairline should circle the bottle completely. And it will—if you rotate the bottle in smooth, steady motions. Turn the bottle as far as possible with each movement. Apply uniform gentle pressure as you turn. If the bottle is rotated in jerky motions, it will leave gaps in the etch and cause deeper etches on some parts of the bottle. When it comes time to complete the fracture, the gaps will not break and the deeper etches will splinter and crack.

Stop scribing when the revolution is finished. *Never cut over a part that has already been scribed.* Recutting the original scribe line will chip the edges and dull the cutting wheel. (If you should skip a spot, place the cutter against the uncut spot and scribe only that part.)

Soon your ears will quickly tell you if you are scribing correctly. For a continuous, clean hairline cut makes a light tearing sound . . . like ripping tissue paper. If the sound stops, you'll know you've skipped a spot. If the tearing sound becomes loud, you'll know you're applying too much pressure. If the "rip" turns into a "crunch," you'll know you've reached the starting point and it's time to stop.

Some bottle artists oil the cutting blade after every five or six cuts using a light oil such as gun oil, sewing machine oil, and so forth. They find that oil keeps the cutting wheel turning smoothly against the glass. Other bottle artists believe that oil "gums up the works." Dirt and glass fragments stick to the oil, making rotation of the cutting wheel more difficult. Try scribing both with and without oil to see which technique you prefer.

Now comes the telltale part of bottle cutting . . . completing the fracture. For Step 3 will produce a clean, even break only if Steps 1 and 2 were performed with care.

Bottles may be fractured by hammering with a tapper; by alternating temperatures; or by heating with an electric wire.

To separate a bottle with a tapper (scribe-and-tap method), insert the tapper so that the "hammer" end is parallel to the scribed line. Begin tapping in one spot with gentle pressure. Gentle taps will usually fracture nonreturnable bottles. With thicker bottles, you may need to gradually increase the tapping pressure—still in the same spot—until a fracture occurs. You can see the fracture begin: the hairline etch becomes wider, like a pencil line.

One tap of ample pressure will create a fracture about one-half inch long. After this occurs, you may then continue tapping the bottle following the circular scribe. Move the hammer about one-eighth inch ahead of the last fracture as you proceed. When you have completed the circle, check to see that no spot has gone unfractured. If you have missed a spot, retap it. The bottle should now readily come apart.

To separate a bottle with alternating temperatures (scribe-and-heat manual method), first hold the etched line over candle flame. Rotate the bottle slowly three or four times about a quarter inch away from the flame. Then, before the bottle cools, stand it upright and rub an ice cube along the scribe line until a crack develops. If the glass has been properly heated, a crack should start the instant the ice touches the bottle. The fracture will continue as the ice is moved along the scribe line.

If the fracture doesn't develop or if the two sections won't now part with a slight tug, simply repeat the procedure until they do.

When alternating temperatures, you complete the fracture by expanding and contracting the glass molecules until a break occurs. Following the same principle, you may also alternate temperatures by holding the bottle under hot then cold running water.

To separate a bottle with an electric wire (scribe-and-heat electric method), place the bottle in its cradle with the scribe line resting at the edge of the cradle. Slip the wire loop over the scribe line and keep the wire tight by pressing the tension lever. Then, hold the "on" button down until a popping, crackling sound tells you the glass is fracturing (this should occur within a few seconds with normal bottles). Rotate the bottle a half turn and repeat. The bottle may now separate by itself, or you may need to rap the scribe line gently with a knife or screwdriver handle.

The heated wire completes the fracture by expanding the glass molecules until the break occurs. The amount of heat required will depend upon the thickness of the glass. Therefore, you will hold the "on" button down longer

Cutting a bottle may take less than two minutes from start to finish. (Demonstrated by Ila Mae Robinson.)

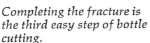

Completing the fracture is the third easy step of bottle cutting.

when fracturing thick champagne bottles or very wide jugs. (The wire loop may be adjusted to fit any size bottle.) The bottle will be heated sufficiently when you can see a visible fracture 180° around the bottle.

Although it is not necessary to scribe a bottle when using the wire-cutting method, some bottle artists prefer to first scribe the bottle, then use the electric wire to complete the fracture. The method is very similar to that just described.

During the fracturing process, do take care not to put your eyes near the cracking glass. You can easily see from a safe distance whether or not the glass is breaking. Or, wait to look until you are through tapping, heating, or cooling. If, however, you wear safety goggles you may watch as closely as you like without fear of flying glass fragments.

After all these detailed instructions, you may begin to wonder if bottle cutting really is easy. Yes! Most bottles are scribed and separated within two minutes. So start practicing. After a few trials and errors, you'll soon discover how fun and simple the hobby of creative bottle cutting can be!

How to Make Rings

An excellent way to practice scribing and fracturing skills is to cut rings from bottles. Instead of using a whole bottle to make just one cut, you can make half a dozen cuts. And you can use the resulting narrow rings for handles, picture frames, wind chimes, mobiles, room dividers, and much more. Here's how.

Scribe the bottle at regularly spaced intervals. Begin scribing at the base of the bottle and work your way up. Next, complete the fracture—again working your way from bottom to top.

At first, only one or two rings may turn out satisfactorily. With practice, however, every cut may be perfect. The rings may then be used in a chain; the top can become part of a set of wind chimes; and the base can be decorated for adornment on a Christmas tree.

Scribe bottle at regularly spaced intervals.

Complete the fracture working from bottom to top.

One bottle thus provides the raw material for many creative projects. (Demonstrated by Ila Mae Robinson.)

Coping with "Problem" Bottles

Average-size round bottles with smooth surfaces are easiest to cut, simple to find, and are most commonly used. The day may come, however, when you wish to cut a bottle that presents more problems.

For example, bottles with dimensional designs can seldom be cut satisfactorily. The reason is that bumpy surfaces will cause the cutter to skip and jump so that a smooth, even hairline is impossible to scribe. But a bottle with a design is beautiful. When cut, it looks like professionally molded glassware. You can cope with this type of bottle by cutting either above or below the dimensional design.

Bottles with unusual shapes, such as square or octagon, also cause cutters to skip and jump. These bottles are best cut with the wire-cutting method or with a plain glass cutter. Remove the cutter from the frame of a scribe-and-tap method kit or buy an inexpensive glass cutter from the hardware store. Use a tin can or block of wood to brace the cutter at the desired height against the

Cut above or below a design molded in the glass, never on top.

bottle. Hold the cutter firmly in place. With your other hand, slowly rotate the bottle against the cutter with as uniformly gentle pressure as possible. Complete the fracture as usual, and cross your fingers for luck!

A bottle with a very large diameter (gallon size or larger) or a very small diameter (two inches minimum) may cause momentary problems for bottle artists using the scribe-and-heat method. The problem is that the cutting wheel will not hit the bottle correctly. Simply loosen the cutting screwhead and readjust the cutting wheel so the blade fits against the glass when the bottle is placed in the cradle.

Wide-mouthed bottles, such as canning jars, may present a problem to bottle artists using the scribe-and-tap method. The pivot cone is too small to fit in a wide neck. This is easily overcome by punching a hole in the lid of the jar (use screwdriver or ice pick) and fitting the cone (or cone bolt) in the hole. Or, drill a hole in the center of a piece of Masonite or plywood. Tape this improvised lid to the bottle and use the hole as a pivot point.

Unusually shaped bottles may be cut with a plain glass cutter . . . and a great deal of luck!

If a bottle neck is too wide for the pivot cone, punch a hole in the lid to hold the cone or cone bolt in place.

How to Remove Necks

By removing a bottle's neck, you can often enhance its beauty. It's very simple to do, but the results are not as reliable as normal bottle cutting.

First, scribe a line as near the neck as possible. If the cutter cannot be adjusted to fit the neck, then scribe the line with a plain glass cutter as explained with "problem" bottles.

The fracture may then be completed with alternating temperatures or heating with an electric wire. Or, try this technique: Hold the neck under cold running water then quickly dip in a pan of hot water. If the neck doesn't break, then gradually increase the temperature of the hot water. You may heat water on the stove and alternate between cold tap water and the increasingly hotter water. With very thick glass, the hot water may need to reach the boiling point before it will fracture. Never attempt to dip the neck into boiling water without "working up to it," or the neck is sure to shatter unevenly. (Bottle artists who use a tapper to complete fractures may substitute this method whenever the tapper doesn't fit well in a bottle.)

If possible, remove the bottle's bottom or hold the bottle so that hot air can escape through the neck. During the heating process, hot gases build up inside the bottle that may cause the bottle to explode if there is no other way for the gases to escape.

Another way to remove the neck of the bottle is with needle-nose pliers. Grasp the neck of the bottle with the pliers about one-quarter inch deep and break outward. Work your way around the neck of the bottle, breaking as much as desired. Glass will fly when removing necks with pliers, so do wear goggles for eye protection.

An easy way to remove necks is to first hold the scribed line under cold running water.

Then quickly dip in a pan of hot water.

If the neck doesn't break, gradually increase the temperature of hot water.

Eventually the bottle will fracture smoothly around the scribe line.

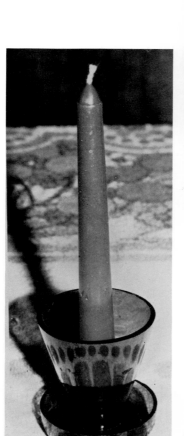

By removing the neck, it may be impossible to guess a "treasure" was once "trash!" (Demonstrated by Ila Mae Robinson.)

How to Drill Holes

Rarely will you need to drill holes in glass. With a drilled hole, however, bottle artists can stack bottles with a rod running through the center (perfect for a lamp base). Bottles may also be used as lampshades when a hole is drilled for the necessary wires to come through. In addition, round globes—such as glass balls—may be cut with the scribe-and-tap method when a hole is drilled for insertion of the pivot cone.

So, if you ever desire to drill a hole, you may do so with either of two methods. The first method follows the example of professional glass cutters by using copper, aluminum, or brass tubing (two to six inches long) in a slow drill press. The tube should be the size of the hole desired. Before drilling, build a dam around the future hole with putty. Fill the dam with water and coarse silicone carbide powder—about grit number 70 to 120 (available from "rock hound" suppliers). With a drill press and dam, it will take about three minutes to cut one-quarter inch of glass, according to the manufacturers of the Fleming Bottle and Jug Cutter.

The second method of drilling holes requires less expensive equipment. Insert a concrete (sometimes called tile) bit into a variable-speed electric drill. Before drilling, chip the glass with a pick or punch so the bit will not slip sideways. If the surface to be drilled is flat or rounded, you will need to build a dam with putty or clay (or even chewing gum!) around the spot to be drilled. Fill the dam with turpentine, which acts as a lubricant and coolant. If the surface to be drilled is concave, however, it will hold the turpentine without a dam. Proceed to drill slowly, carefully, and at a rate of less than 400 rpm. You may enlarge the drilled hole with a three-cornered file and ream using a little turpentine on the file to keep it cool, according to the manufacturers of the Miracle Bottle Cutter.

Either of these methods may be used to drill a hole in the surface of a glass globe or ball. Once the hole is drilled, insert the cone of a scribe-and-tap cutter in the hole (it serves as your pivot point) and scribe where desired. Complete the fracture by alternating temperatures. With this technique, you can easily create unique brandy snifters from Japanese glass floats.

The use of goggles is a wise safety measure whenever drilling glass.

With concave surfaces, a hole may be drilled without a dam.

By using a drilled hole as a pivot point, glass balls may be cut with the scribe-and-tap method. (Created by Ila Mae Robinson.)

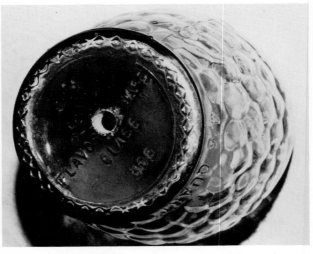

Holes enable bottle artists to create lampshades and bases. (Demonstrated by Yorkshire House, makers of the Miracle Bottle Cutter.)

How to Make Chains

A popular but frustrating project of bottle artists is to create "chains" with rings cut from bottles. This project is popular because it's fun. Plus, the chains may be used as room dividers and novel decorations. But it can be frustrating because rings often shatter completely rather than breaking evenly.

If you have the patience to try this project, however, begin by scribing a line across a ring. (Use a glass cutter from a kit or from the hardware store.) Next, gently rap the scribe with a tapper, knife, or screwdriver until the glass fractures. Then use needle-nose pliers to widen the fracture so that another ring can be inserted through this space. (Hold the ring very carefully or use gloves to protect your hands.)

Scribe and fracture every other ring in the chain. In other words, make a gap in the first ring; slip a second whole ring through that gap; make a gap in the third ring and slip it through the second ring; add a fourth whole ring by slipping it through the gap of the third ring. Continue adding rings until the chain is as long as desired.

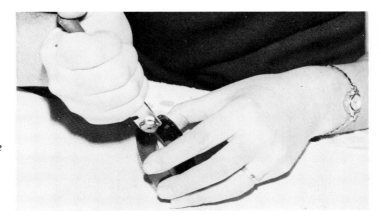

To make a chain of bottle rings, first scribe a line.

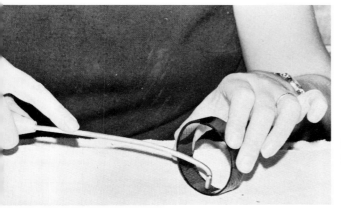

Gently rap the scribed line until it fractures.

Widen the fracture by breaking with needle-nose pliers.

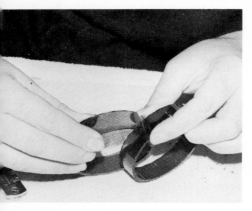

Insert a whole ring into the ring with a gap.

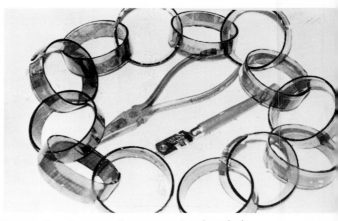

Every other ring must have a gap for the whole ring to slip through. (Demonstrated by Ila Mae Robinson.)

Chains of rings cut from bottles can become fascinating room dividers and novel decorations.

How to Cut Freehand

As you already know, it is easiest to cut a bottle successfully with a bottle cutting kit. Kits provide the most reliable method of cutting a bottle in a straight line. However, if you wish to cut in a curve, at a slant, or in any other irregular direction, you will need to cut freehand.

Instead of being guided by your dependable kit, you will now use a glass cutter guided by your own hand . . . which is not so dependable! In fact, it can be very difficult to scribe a bottle freehand with uniform, continuous gentle pressure. But freehand cutting is fun to try and enables you to create unusual, original bottle art.

Before cutting freehand, you should first cut a set of glasses shown in the next chapter and complete several of the projects shown in subsequent chapters. With this experience, you will learn to recognize the sound and sight of a good hairline scribe. And you will become adept at completing the fracture. Such practice will increase your chances of cutting freehand successfully.

Let's try it. First, draw a line with a felt-tip pen where you want to scribe. Next, follow this line with a glass cutter removed from a scribe-and-tap kit or purchased from the hardware store. Finally, complete the fracture with one of the methods described earlier.

Because it is difficult to obtain a good scribe when cutting freehand, the bottle may fracture in a completely different direction from that which you etched. Or, it may fracture in several directions. But keep trying . . . eventually you'll be able to boast a unique freehand cut!

The first step of freehand cutting is to draw a line which serves as your guide.

Follow the line applying uniform gentle pressure on the cutter.

Complete the fracture as usual.

Freehand cutting enables bottle artists to create unusual, interesting shapes.

By cutting at a slant and adding a handle, you can make a dandy water pitcher. (Created by Ila Mae Robinson.)

Chapter 4

Beginning Project: Glasses

Drinking glasses are the most popular creation of beginning bottle artists. And no wonder . . . a set of six tumblers can easily be completed in half an hour!

Yet glasses require all the "basics" of bottle cutting that you will encounter with more advanced projects. So learn how to make glasses and you can then create any project shown in this book.

Cut-and-Sand Glasses

The simplest set of glasses is made by merely cutting the bottle in one place, then sanding the cut edge smooth.

First, collect a set of matching bottles. Because you will not decorate these glasses, you may wish to select bottles that already have their own designs, interesting shape, attractive labels, or colored glass. (Paper labels may be protected with several coats of acrylic sealer, clear lacquer, or shellac.)

Next, decide how small or tall you wish the glasses to be. For example, eleven-ounce amber beer bottles make excellent milk glasses when cut four or five inches from the base. Clear ketchup bottles are perfect for juice when cut three inches from the base. Or, sixteen-ounce pop bottles are ideal for mixed drinks or iced tea when cut seven or eight inches tall.

Adjust the cutter to the desired height on the first bottle. Do not readjust the cutter until all bottles have been scribed. This insures that all glasses will be the same size.

After the cut has been completed, sand the edges smooth. Glasses require an extremely careful sanding job to prevent cut lips! One very easy method is to rub the glass edge in circular motions on a piece of semifine sandpaper, such as grade 120. When the outside edge is smooth, hold the glass to sand the inside edge. If you spend about ten minutes sanding each glass, the edge should be completely safe for drinking.

Many bottle artists find that emery cloth is superior to sandpaper for obtaining a smooth edge. Still others prefer a wet-and-dry sanding cloth or water. (The water also washes sanding grit down the sink.) Another idea is to paper lubricated with a few drops of thin oil or placed under running tap first use a very coarse sandpaper, such as grade 80, then finish the job with a fine sandpaper, such as grade 220. When finished, you may rub a little vegetable oil into the edges to seal them.

If you own an electric drill, the sanding process may be considerably simplified. Fasten the drill firmly to a bench or in a vise and attach a five- or six-inch sanding disk (buy disks that are marked for "wood, plastic, or glass").

While the disk is turning, hold the bottle's edge firmly against the disk and rotate clockwise slowly. Presto . . . the edge will be smooth in seconds instead of minutes!

Any of these sanding methods will produce a satisfactory edge. And most bottle cutting kits include sanding paper or emery cloth. Experiment to see which sanding procedure you prefer.

Sand the outside edge by rubbing in circular motions.

As an extra precaution, sand the inside edge.

Electric drills with sanding attachments can simplify the sanding process.

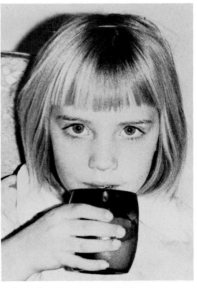

Simple cut-and-sand glasses are perfect for children.

Labels may be left on bottles if protected with acrylic sealer, clear lacquer, or shellac.

Bottles with a design make attractive tumblers.

Painted labels create a "mod" set of glasses for mixed drinks or iced tea.

Look for bottles with unusual shapes for cut-and-sand glasses.

Cut-and-Glue Glasses

One more step—gluing—can transform cut-and-sand glasses into attractively shaped goblets. Shapes are as limitless as the kinds of bottles available and your imagination!

For example, you may cut a bottle an inch or less from the base. Turn the top of the bottle upside down and glue to the base. Instantly you've created an ideal glass for lemonade or root beer floats.

Or, cut the bottle a few inches below the neck. Then glue the bottom of the glass to the top of the neck. This goblet will be dandy for drinking beer.

By cutting the bottle at top or bottom in different proportions, you can create a variety of goblets. Be sure to sand *both* cut edges before gluing. (Bases that aren't sanded may scratch table- or countertops.)

Now, a word about glue. It is recommended that you use either epoxy or a waterproof adhesive—such as Dow Corning's Silicone Adhesive—to protect the goblet through many washings. Epoxies made for marine use are also excellent due to their waterproof qualities. In addition, quick-drying epoxies that enable you to use the goblet within minutes are now on the market.

Much care should be taken when joining bottle parts together, for a sloppy job can result in leakage or a goblet that eventually comes apart. For best results, lightly sand the edges to be joined with sandpaper or emery cloth. Apply the adhesive or epoxy in ample amounts to a clean surface. Place the top on the base, and let settle of its own accord. In other words, don't force the parts together. Excess adhesive will seep out. Let the goblet dry undisturbed overnight (unless you use quick-drying epoxy). You may then remove the excess glue with fingernail or razor blade.

By applying silicone adhesive or epoxy with care, you can be assured that your goblets will provide years of use.

For best adhesion, sand edges to be glued.

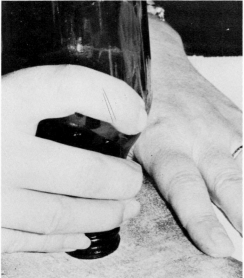

Apply an ample amount of silicone adhesive or epoxy.

Let the two parts settle together and dry overnight.

Remove excess adhesive with fingernail or razor blade.

Bottle bottoms glued to necks are dandy for beer drinkers.

A bottle top glued to the base is ideal for serving lemonade.

With instructions presented so far, you can now create three differently shaped glasses from the same bottle!

Cut-and-Decorate Glasses

Bottle cutting really becomes an "art" when you decorate the glasses you have cut. Until now, the glasses you have created may be easily identified as bottles. But a few decorative touches can make your glasses really professional looking. Your investment will be only a few pennies for decals or paint!

Let's start with decals, which can be found in any variety store. After the bottles have been cut and sanded, apply suitable decals according to the manufacturer's instructions. The decal should be applied to the outside of the glass; and, if the decal is not waterproof, it should be protected with acrylic sealer, clear lacquer, or shellac.

Consider decals that match or are similar in design. For example, matching eagles are impressive on tall clear glasses to be used for cool summer drinks. Decals of similar animals are colorful on clear ketchup bottles cut into milk glasses for children. Use matching flowers or similar fruit to decorate juice glasses.

For an "extra" professional touch to glasses with decals, paint the rim of the glass. Use a waterproof craft paint available in hobby stores. Gold and silver paints are particularly lovely, although a white or colored rim may be preferred to blend with a color in the decal. When painting the rim, maintain a straight line by first applying masking tape. Then you may paint without fear of zigzag lines. When the paint is dry, remove the masking tape. Your set of decorator glasses is now complete!

Decals should be applied to the outside of the glass.

Inexpensive decals create professional-looking glasses.

Masking tape insures a straight line around the rim.

Colorful animal decals will delight wee ones.

Another easy way to decorate glass sets is to add painted designs. No talent is needed because you can simply trace a design with ball-point paint tubes. Here's how it works.

Find a design you like among embroidery patterns, greeting cards, magazine illustrations, and so forth. Cut the design to fit inside the glass and affix with masking tape. Then copy the design by outlining with ball-point paint tubes. (Such paints are available in hobby stores or in the embroidery section of variety and syndicate stores.) The design may be filled in with color or left as an outline only. Next, waterproof the design by baking the painted glass for about an hour in a slow (250°) oven. When the oven has completely cooled, remove the glasses. You'll now own a set of tumblers as colorful and bright as those sold in department stores!

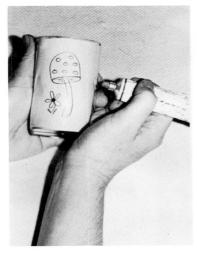

Use masking tape to keep design in place.

Copy design on outside of glass with ball-point paint tubes.

Waterproof the design by baking in a slow oven.

Still another way to decorate your glasses is to add a handle. The handle may also be made of bottles. For example, handles created from whole rings or half rings transform the glass into a mug.

To make a half ring, scribe a whole ring in two parallel places. Tap the scribed line gently with tapper or screwdriver to fracture. Thus, you create two handles at the same time!

Sand whole or half rings smooth, then glue to the glass, using gluing procedures explained under Cut-and-Glue Glasses.

Many bottle artists find that handles made from bottles are not easily grasped, they look out of proportion to the glass itself, or in time they become unglued.

For this reason, you may wish to improvise your own handle. Drawer pulls may be attached with glue and/or copper wire. Wooden handles can be easily made out of dowels, broomsticks, or discarded thread spools.

Generally speaking, however, most handles will not hold up under constant use. So it is recommended that handles be used with a tender touch or else for decorative purposes only.

A bottle ring glued to a glass creates a novel mug.

Half rings are easily made with a scribe and a tap.

Drawer pulls may be glued on, then secured with copper wire.

Wooden handles can be made from dowels, broomsticks, or thread spools.

Chapter 5

Creative Kitchenware

What better place is there to start creative bottle cutting than in the kitchen? After all, the very bottles that are used in the kitchen can be transformed into no-cost serving dishes, decorative planters, and everyday utilitarian items. The ideas for kitchenware are endless...here's just a sampling to tickle your imagination.

Bowls from Bottles

Once you learn to cut bottles, you need never buy another bowl! With just one cut, a bit of sanding, and perhaps added decoration, you can create bowls to hold cereal, fruit, soup, dessert, sugar, and much, much more.

As with glasses, the prettiest bowls are made from bottles with unusual shapes, colored glass, or raised surfaces. For example, the toothpick bowl shown only required one simple cut. But, because the bottle artist selected a small green lemon juice bottle with a raised surface, the bowl looks like professionally cut glass!

Often you can find products that come in matching bottles of various sizes that enable you to create a whole set of bowls. Using a half-gallon wine bottle for a serving bowl and "fifth" wine bottles for eating bowls, one artist made a lovely set that's perfect for salad, fruit, and dessert.

Bottles and jugs with ready-made designs lend themselves to a bit of "fancying-up." A gallon jug with an apple design, for instance, can be charming when the design is enhanced with paint, as shown. Use regular enamel paint after first sanding the surface to be painted. (Glass is so slick that enamel will not adhere well unless you sand.)

Or, you may use paint that is especially made to adhere to glass. Available at hobby stores and in hobby sections of variety stores, there are two kinds of glass paints: the type that crystallizes upon application and the type that merely stains the glass. To decorate the grape design on the bowls illustrated, a crystallizing glass paint was selected for the leaves and a staining glass paint was used for the grapes. When using glass paints, allow each color to dry (ten to twenty minutes) before adding the next color if the colors overlap. Like all lacquers, glass paints should be applied to a clean surface in a well-ventilated room.

Glass paints may be waterproofed by spraying with an acrylic sealer. Unless the sealer is sprayed gently from a proper distance, it will dissolve the pattern of crystallizing paints. Thus, you would be wise to practice spraying the sealer on a discarded bottle before spraying your "treasure."

Another way to decorate bowls is with decals. Although decals are lovely, inexpensive, and easy to apply, be extra careful when selecting colors. A fruit decal can look "washed out" when real fruit is placed in the bowl. So select colors that will not have to compete with the "real thing."

Bottles with raised surfaces can look like professionally cut glass. (Created by Ila Mae Robinson.)

Enamel may be applied to glass for decorative accents if the glass is first sanded. (Created by Alberta Bainter.)

Matching bottles in various sizes can be cut into coordinated sets. (Created by Ila Mae Robinson.)

Special glass paint will crystallize into intriguing patterns as it dries. (Courtesy Fry Plastics International, Inc., makers of Cryst-L-Craze.)

Glass paints are particularly nice on bottles with "ready-made" designs.

Decals are easy to apply, yet give bowls more eye appeal.

When colors overlap, allow each color to dry before adding the next color.

Canisters and Other Keepers

A nifty way to keep food fresh and show off your bottle art is to create food containers that may be displayed on countertops.

Canisters are a favorite of bottle artists. They may be cut from bottles ranging in size from large to small. For example, you could use a gallon jug, half-gallon jug, a cooking oil bottle, and juice bottle. Another idea is use all gallon jugs, cutting each jug consecutively lower. Canisters cut from the same size jugs may be stacked on countertops.

Lids for canisters may be cut from plywood with a coping saw. Measure the mouth of the canister, then cut one piece of quarter-inch plywood to fit and another piece an inch larger. Glue the two pieces together. The smaller piece will fit snugly in the canister's opening; and the larger piece will prevent air from entering. Glue or screw on a handle. Quite often you will be able to find lids that already fit your canisters, such as plastic lids from coffee cans.

Canisters are easily decorated with ball-point paint tubes and decals. Use colors that coordinate with your kitchen's decor.

Another fun-to-make food keeper is a cookie jar. The jar shown was created from two gallon jugs. The first jug was cut eight inches from the bottom. The second jug was cut one and a half inches from the bottom, then turned upside down to make a lid. A plastic drawer knob was glued on to serve as a handle. Finally, a design was applied with a ball-point paint tube.

Even cheese savers may be created from bottles. Cut a gallon or half-gallon jug the desired height, then turn upside down. Glue on a handle and place over a wooden circle cut from hardwood. Or, use an inverted wooden salad bowl as the base of your cheese saver.

Simple one-cut food keepers are also eye catching as well as practical. Spice jars, for example, may be cut from narrow seasoning bottles and capped with a cork. A decal of the spice it contains can transform a beer bottle into a spice jar. Larger bottles with small necks can be sealed with a cork and used to hold tea, baking soda, salt, and such. Corks can be found in variety stores for less than a nickel!

Canisters may be cut from bottles and jugs of various sizes. (Created by Ila Mae Robinson.)

Gallon jugs make ideal cookie jars. (Created by Ila Mae Robinson.)

Cheese stays fresh and moist beneath a cut jug.

Small bottles are easily transformed into spice jars with one cut.

A narrow-mouthed bottle and cork can hold any kitchen staple.

Cooking Aids

Bottle art can also produce extremely practical kitchenware. For example, two liquor bottles can be cut in half and glued together to make a rolling pin. Bottle and jug tops are ideal funnels. And even the most common bottle can be used for a gelatin mold.

Other cooking aids you may wish to try are storage and blender jars. Using wide-mouthed canning jars, cut the jar in half and top with a plastic coffee can lid...presto, a perfect small container for leftovers. Some canning and mayonnaise jars may screw into your blender. Cut these jars in half, turn upside down (so the grooves fit into the blender), and top with a plastic lid. Such small blender jars are perfect for mixing small amounts as well as for storage.

Speaking of practical ideas, don't overlook the possibility of using bottle art to replace broken items. When a glass breaks in a set of tumblers, for instance, you may be able to duplicate the glass with a cut bottle. Bottles may also be used to replace broken glass jars in humidors, chimneys of kerosene camping lanterns, ashtrays in smoking stands, and so forth.

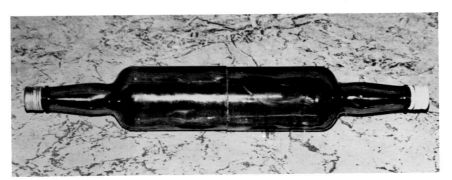

Rolling pins may be as small or large as you desire when you make your own.

Tops cut from bottles make perfect funnels.

Even a plain bottle makes a dandy dish or mold for gelatin.

Dessert Dishes

Ice cream sundaes, parfaits, and other tempting taste treats deserve their own special dish. With two cuts and a dab of glue, any bottle may be transformed into a dessert goblet.

First, cut the bottom of the bottle—this will be used as the base. Next, cut the top of the bottle, which will be turned upside down and glued to the

Cut the top and bottom from a bottle to make a dessert dish.

Invert top and glue to base.

Fill with taste-tempting treats. (Created by Ila Mae Robinson.)

base. When determining where to cut the top of the bottle, keep in mind how it will look when finished and how much dessert you want the dish to hold. The remaining center section of the bottle may be discarded or saved for another project.

Create a dessert set from differently shaped bottles for variety or create a matched set of goblets. Either set is sure to please when filled with yummies.

Planters Aplenty

Windowsills and countertops are easily perked up with the addition of potted plants and flowers. Just for fun, select bottles that hold products used in the kitchen to create your planters.

For example, the lowly ketchup bottle may be cut into a vase and enhanced with gold trim. Or, yesterday's syrup bottle may be transformed into today's planter by cutting the bottom and then gluing the bottom to the bottle's neck. Still another idea is to glue several bottle bottoms together, letting the top bottle serve as a planter.

Ideas for kitchen planters and vases are endless. Browse the garbage to see what you can invent!

ovel kitchen bottles make e-catching planters. reated by Donald Rader.)

Stack and glue several bottle bottoms into a graceful arrangement. (Created by Donald Rader.)

Ketchup bottles become elegant vases when cut and trimmed with gold. (Created by Ila Mae Robinson.)

Relish Dishes

Here are two creative bottle cutting ideas you're sure to relish...because both ideas may be used for relish!

The first relish dish is easily created by cutting three bottles in equal heights. Glue the bottles together. Then, cut a matching ring to serve as a handle and glue in the center of the three bottles. Let dry overnight. This clever dish may be used to serve mayonnaise, ketchup, and mustard, or a choice of salad dressings.

The second relish dish requires freehand cutting and a great deal of luck! The jug must be cut vertically on both sides from top to bottom and on the bottom. Use a glass cutter from the hardware store or remove the cutter from the frame of a scribe-and-tap-kit. Masking tape may be used as a guide for the scribe line. Pull the cutter along the edge of the masking tape trying to create a hairline etch. Apply uniform pressure.

After scribing the entire jug, complete the fracture by holding the jug under alternately hot and cold running water. Or, hold the scribe line over a candle, then rub with an ice cube. Continue alternating temperatures until the jug breaks. Because freehand cutting is very unpredictable, the jug may not break as desired. But trying is half the fun, and eventually you'll be rewarded with a truly novel relish dish!

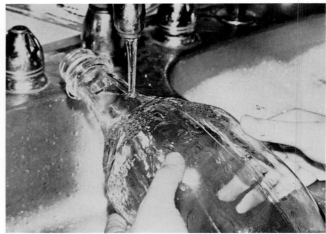

Complete the fracture with alternating temperatures.

Masking tape can guide freehand scribing.

With luck, the jug will break in half. Sand and use as a relish dish. (Created by Alberta Bainter.)

This clever creation is perfect for relishes and salad dressings.

Serving Sets

Bottle cutting kits will continue to pay for themselves many times over with the money you save on household goods. In fact, you need never buy another dish. Instead, let discarded bottles provide the basis for matching serving sets.

Gallon jugs can be cut low to become small breakfast and luncheon plates. Or, create a sectioned dinner plate by cutting three half-gallon jugs as close to the bottom as possible. Glue the three bottoms together in a circle. Use the separate sections to hold meat, potatoes, and vegetables.

Half-gallon jugs make dandy bowls for soup and cereal. Smaller bottles may be made into glasses. Tiny bottles can be transformed into eggcups, toothpick holders, sugar bowls, and other items. Even napkin rings may be cut from bottles!

Serving dishes cut from bottles and jugs are excellent for use on the patio or for use by small children. Who cares if a plate is broken? You can replace it in two minutes at absolutely no cost!

Clear glass bottles and jugs were used to create a no-cost breakfast set.

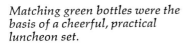

Matching green bottles were the basis of a cheerful, practical luncheon set.

Chapter 6

Party Room Possibilities

Bottles containing refreshments for the party room are easily cut into festive accessories for this happy place. The possibilities are endless. For example, you can make a complete set of bar glasses from liquor bottles by simply cutting at different heights. "Fifth" liquor bottles may be cut three inches high to serve drinks "on the rocks"—or cut six inches high to serve mixed cocktails.

Glasses are only the beginning, however. With a little imagination, you can fill your party room with ashtrays, coasters, lamps, decorations, and much more. Try it!

Ashtrays

The bottom of any bottle can be cut about an inch high to become an ashtray. Use the bottoms of gallon jugs for heavy smokers. Or, cut a six-pack of amber beer bottles into an attractive matched set of ashrays.

Even clear glass ashtrays can look professional if you add a decal to perk up its plain appearance. Place the decal on the underneath side of the ashtray so it won't be charred by burning cigarettes.

Another idea is to borrow techniques learned under Cut-and-Glue Glasses (chapter 4) to create stemmed ashtrays. Or, glue a regular ashtray to the neck of a cut bottle.

Cigar smokers will appreciate larger ashtrays, of course. Please them with an ashtray created from a bottle cut vertically. Refer to Relish Dishes (chapter 5) for complete instructions.

Matching sets of ashtrays are easily cut from green wine bottles or amber beer bottles. (Created by Ila Mae Robinson.)

Even clear glass bottles can become attractive ashtrays with the addition of a decal.

A bit of glue transforms ordinary ashtrays into novel stemware. (Created by Yorkshire House, makers of the Miracle Bottle Cutter.)

Cut a bottle vertically to please cigar smokers. (Created by Alberta Bainter.)

Candle Holders

Subtle lighting and pleasant aromas can enhance your party room when you create candle holders for colorful scented candles.

Let your imagination soar...the variety of differently shaped candle holders you can cut from bottles is limitless. If you use a cut bottle for the base of your candle holder, be sure to sand its edge as smoothly as you sand the cup. Otherwise, the base might scratch furniture.

Browse the candle holders pictured for ideas. Try to duplicate what you see or—better yet—try to invent original holders of your own.

Look for bottles with unusual shapes or designs to hold candles. (Created by Donald Rader.)

Safe from drafts, this candle will burn for hours in its "chimney" made from two ketchup bottle tops. (Created by Ila Mae Robinson.)

Cut and discard the midsection of a bottle; glue top and base together. The result is a holder that's just the right size for tapered candles. (Created by Edward Parker.)

Scented candles are novel party room decorations when placed in holders cut from beer bottles. (Created by Donald Rader.)

Gracefully shaped candle holders are easily made from five beer bottle tops. Use an inverted ashtray as the base. (Created by Yorkshire House, makers of the Miracle Bottle Cutter.)

For a change, use a bottle bottom in its normal position rather than turning upside down for a base. (Created by Ila Mae Robinson.)

Coasters

Coasters cut from bottle bottoms will be the perfect complement for glasses you have also cut from bottles!

Simply select a bottle for the coaster that is a bit larger than the bottle used for the glass. For example, when making coasters for glasses cut from beer bottles, use "fifth" wine or liquor bottles. When making coasters for glasses cut from wine or liquor bottles, use half-gallon jugs.

Although a set of matching coasters cut from colored bottles is very attractive, you may wish to add a bit of decoration. As with ashtrays, decals can perk up clear glass coasters. Or use ball-point paint tubes to make your own design (Cut-and-Decorate Glasses, chapter 4.) Or merely trim the cut edge of the coaster with waterproof gold paint, craft lead, or filigree.

Another clever idea is to cushion coasters with colorful yarn, raffia, or macramé cord. Apply a ring of white glue to the outside bottom of the coaster and wind the cord in place. Continue to add glue and wind the cord until the bottom of the coaster is covered. Follow the same procedure on the side of the coaster. Let dry overnight before using.

Starting with the outside edge of the coaster's bottom, apply glue, then wind the cord.

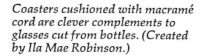

Coasters cushioned with macramé cord are clever complements to glasses cut from bottles. (Created by Ila Mae Robinson.)

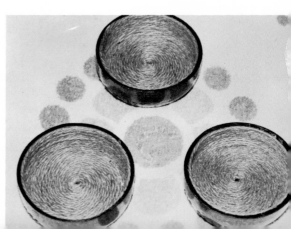

Coasters decorated with macramé cord by Ila Mae Robinson.

Matching bowl set by Ila Mae Robinson.

Three elaborate candelabra made from beverage bottles by Donald Rader.

Freehand cut wine bottle.

Candle holders made from different bottle parts by Ila Mae Robinson.

Canister set cut from different sized bottles and jugs by Ila Mae Robinson.

Hanging planter made from wine bottle and raffia by Ila Mae Robinson.

Mobile made from driftwood and glass rings (far right).

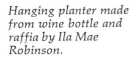

Cigar ashtray cut vertically freehand by Alberta Bainter.

Beer mug with handle.

Bowls decorated with glass paints.

Patchwork lamp made from two juice jugs, fabric, and craft metal by Alberta Bainter.

Mediterranean-style candle holder in metal base by Arberta Lammers.

Soap dish, water glass, and wastebasket decorated for bathroom.

Keepsake preserved in clear liquor bottle.

Wind chimes made from bottle tops by Ila Mae Robinson.

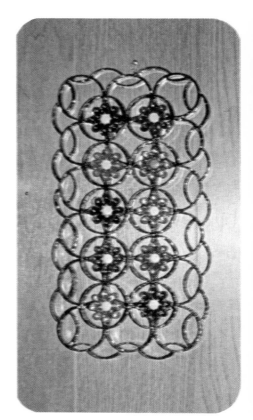

Ornate wall plaque created from bottle rings and molded plastic flowers by Donald Rader.

Bottle rings and bottoms decorated into scene ornaments for Christmas tree by Arberta Lammers.

Desk set created with crystallizing glass paints by Ila Mae Robinson.

Wedding mug created with crystallizing paints and white trim.

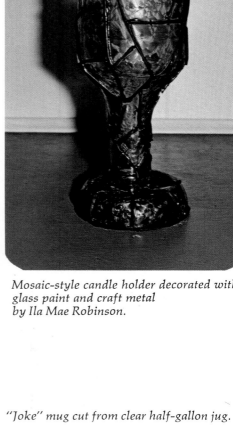

Mosaic-style candle holder decorated with glass paint and craft metal by Ila Mae Robinson.

"Joke" mug cut from clear half-gallon jug.

Ice chest made with three jugs, rug padding, and drawer pull by Ila Mae Robinson.

Breakfast dishes created from clear glass bottles.

Fishbowls

Any gallon or half-gallon jug can easily become a fishbowl. Just cut, sand, and then move the fish into its new home. Add crushed rock for more color. Or, suspend the bowl in a macramé net for a hanging fishbowl.

Check with a pet store to learn how many fish can safely live in a certain size bowl and to learn the best procedure for transferring the fish into its new home cut from a bottle!

Half-gallon and gallon jugs make ideal fishbowls.

Crushed rock adds color to your fish's new home.

Cut three jugs into the desired size.

Glue a drawer pull to the top of an inverted jug bottom. Ice stays frozen for hours. (Created by Ila Mae Robinson.)

Assemble the gallon jug, rug padding, and half-gallon jug.

Ice Chests

Remove the top of a gallon jug to make an ice holder for a party room. The resulting holder may be used as it is; it may be decorated with decals or paint; or it may be used to replace cracked insulation in an ice chest you already own.

Or, you can make a more creative ice chest with the following supplies: two gallon jugs, one half-gallon jug, a drawer pull, and rug padding. Cut one gallon jug and the half-gallon jug as close to the top as possible. Cut the other gallon jug about an inch and a half from the base. Line the inside of the gallon jug with rug padding and insert the half-gallon jug. Next, glue the drawer pull to the inverted bottom of the second gallon jug, which will become the lid.

The rug padding serves as insulation to keep ice cubes frozen for hours. Guests in your party room will be amazed to learn you created this unusual ice chest from bottles!

Jiggers

Looking for a quick and easy project? Simply cut a tiny bottle and glue the bottom to the neck. You'll have an "instant" jigger!

If you want the jigger to measure accurately, fill a commercial jigger with water and pour into the bottle before cutting. Mark the bottle at the waterline and cut accordingly. The fun of making your own jiggers, however, is that you can cut them smaller for dainty thirsts or larger to satisfy king-size thirsts.

Jiggers cut from tiny bottles can be as cute and accurate as commercial jiggers.

Lights

Leftover wine bottles become dandy lights over party room bars. And you can make one yourself with about a dollar's worth of electrical supplies. Here's what's needed: a light bulb, socket, electrical wire, and plug-in. You may

Electrify wine bottles with a receptacle, cord and plug . . . about a dollar's worth of supplies!

Greenish wine bottles or amber beer bottles cast a soft light above party room bars.

also wish to add a threaded rod to hold the wire in place or a toggle switch to turn the light on and off rather than pulling the plug.

If in doubt about how to electrify a wine bottle, take the cut bottle to the hardware store and tell the salesman there what you wish to do. He can show you exactly how to do it. Chances are, he may even electrify the bottle for you because it takes only a few minutes.

Mobiles

A mobile—a construction of delicately balanced movable parts—is sure to be a conversation piece in any party room. Mobiles may be made entirely of bottle parts or bottle parts may be combined with driftwood, beads, molded plastic figures, or designs cut from metal.

The trick is to balance these parts so that each part is suspended gracefully into space. Start at the top and add glass rings and/or other materials, balancing each part as you proceed.

In the process, you'll discover a few basic laws of gravity! For example, if you hang two bottle rings of equal weight an equal distance from the center of a piece of driftwood, both rings will be balanced. But, if you vary any of these conditions, one ring will hang lower than the other. That's the fun of making a mobile . . . to see what works!

String, yarn, copper wire—any flexible strand may be used to tie one part to another. Glue the string in place so it won't slip. If the party room has soft lighting, use transparent fish line on your mobile. The line will "disappear," making the mobile seem truly suspended in space.

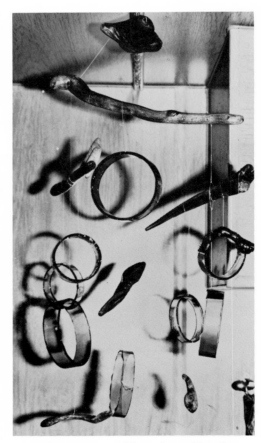

Bottle rings are tinkly and twinkly when hung in a mobile.

Mugs for Fun

Decorative mugs can add color and perhaps a few chuckles to a party room. Easy to make, mugs require only one cut, careful sanding (if it will be used for drinking), and a dab of glue. Popular bottles for mugs are clear half-gallon jugs, colored wine and liquor bottles, and quart-size beer bottles.

If you have a favorite brand of alcoholic beverage, use this bottle with its label intact. Protect the label with several coats of acrylic sealer, clear lacquer, or shellac.

Mugs may also be decorated with designs squeezed from tubes containing craft lead. Or, if the bottle has a design molded in the glass, enhance the design with waterproof gold paint.

Another idea: Create a novelty mug with "joke" lettering. On very large mugs, for example, you could write "Bet 'Cha Can't" or "Johnson's Jigger" with glitter. First, write the letters with a felt-tip pen; then follow these letters with white glue; finally sprinkle glitter over the glue. Let dry and shake off excess glitter.

Members of your family or frequent guests might also enjoy their own personalized mugs. Write their names with glitter, paint and brush, or ball-point paint tubes.

Protect labels from favorite beverages with acrylic sealer, clear lacquer, or shellac. (Created by Dirk McCurdy.)

Metal designs may be squeezed from tubes containing gold, silver, lead, or steel.

Add a "fancy" flavor to mugs with waterproof gold paint.

Bottles with designs already molded in the glass are ideal subjects for a touch of gold paint. (Created by Alberta Bainter.)

Mugs are easily personalized with ball-point paint tubes. (Created by Ila Mae Robinson.)

Half-gallon mugs are cute with "joke" lettering.

Party Sets

If you want to really impress your guests, create a coordinated party set with bottle art. It's very simple. Just use the same type of bottle to make mugs, ashtrays, cigarette containers, and such. Leave the labels on, and they'll all match!

Remember, it is not possible to cut over a label. So cut either above or below. It may be necessary to remove labels then replace them to achieve the desired height. For example, on the cigarette container shown, the label was too high. The bottle artist soaked the bottle in warm sudsy water until the glue loosened and the label could be removed without harm. After the bottle was cut, the label was replaced and reglued at a lower height.

Coordinated party sets are certain to impress guests.

Chapter 7

Living Room
Luxuries

Bottle art in the living room can be so ornate, so creative, that you can now own luxuries that you might not otherwise afford. A good example is living room lamps. With discarded jugs, glass paint, and craft metal, bottle artists can make Tiffany-style lamps that sometimes sell for up to fifty dollars in department stores. Similarly, you can duplicate elegant candy dishes that cost a small fortune in gift shops.

Thus, when you create luxuries for the living room, you will truly turn trash to treasure!

Candelabra

If you have already made a few simple candle holders for the party room, perhaps you're ready to test your skill and patience on an elaborate candelabrum for the living room. Candelabra designed to hold three or more candles require an ample supply of matching bottles, a strong, reliable epoxy; a sense of balance and proportion on the part of the bottle artist; and up to a week's time to assemble.

By now you have the skill to cut all the bottles required in the candelabra pictured here. Now see if you have the patience! First, select a base. The base bottle should be larger than succeeding bottles and be heavy enough to balance the weight of candelabrum arms. The base bottle may be filled with crushed rock or salt for additional weight.

Next, add the bottle parts that will support the arms. Use whole rings and half rings cut from identically colored bottles for "bracing" as well as looks. Allow the epoxy to dry overnight before adding more bottle parts (and therefore more stress).

Now complete the top half before gluing to the base. Cut three, four, or more bottles (depending upon how many arms you desire) at the bottom to use for arms. Lay them horizontally and glue to a vertical bottle in the center. Add a ring, bottom, and bottle top to the arm to hold the candle. If you desire another candle holder in the center, add a vertical bottle, bottom, and top.

Remember to let each additional bottle part dry thoroughly after gluing. When completely dry, glue to the base. Use more bottle rings and half rings to brace the arms. Think of your candelabrum as a bridge . . . it must have proper support and balance or it will topple.

Because of the many bottles you must cut and the drying period between each gluing, it will take many days to complete this project. But, as you can see, your efforts will certainly be worthwhile!

First complete the base for the candelabrum . . . the heavier, the better. (Created by Donald Rader.)

Use whole rings and half rings for additional support as well as looks. (Created by Donald Rader.)

Candelabrum arms and holders were made from matching amber beer bottles. (Created by Donald Rader.)

Large scented candles may be placed in holders cut from quart-size juice bottles. (Created by Alberta Bainter.)

A painted bottle top glued to a metal base blends with Mediterranean-style living rooms. (Created by Arberta Lammers.)

Flame burning behind painted glass casts intriguing patterns. (Courtesy Fry Plastics International, Inc., makers of Cryst-L-Craze.)

Holders for large and scented candles can be made with much less effort than candelabra for tapered candles. In fact, you can create graceful, colorful candle holders with just one cut and glass paint in less than five minutes!

Simply select a gracefully shaped clear glass bottle and cut at the desired height. You can remove the top, invert, and glue to a metal base. You can cut the bottle twice, using the neck for a stem and the bottom for a cup. Or, glue several bottles together and balance the holder on top.

No matter which shape you prefer, you'll find that glass paint truly transforms plain glass bottles into works of art. Select a paint that stains or crystallizes (see Bowls from Bottles, chapter 5) and coordinates with the living room color scheme. As the flame burns, it dances behind the painted glass casting different patterns.

Glass paint can also be combined with craft metal to create a luxurious "mosaic" candle holder. Mosaic designs are not only beautiful and easy to make, but are perhaps one of the most "fun" projects of bottle artists.

First, draw random shapes on a clear glass bottle with a felt-tip pen. Then follow the lines you have drawn with craft metal (such as Liquid Lead or MagiCraft Craft Lead). Try to squeeze and pull the craft metal tube in a smooth, continuous motion so that the lead follows as uniformly as possible.

When the leading has dried, fill in the resulting designs with a staining or crystallizing glass paint. Use at least three differently colored paints. Bold colors—such as green, red, blue, purple—are particularly attractive.

To create a mosaic candle
holder, first draw random
designs on the glass.

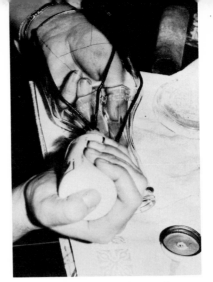

Gently squeeze craft metal
along the lines you have drawn.

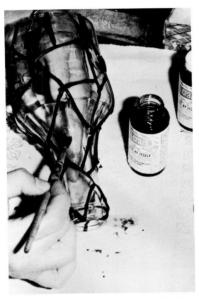

When the leading has dried, fill
in the designs with glass paints.

Mosaic candle holders add
luxurious accents to living room
decor. (Created by Ila Mae
Robinson.)

Candy Dishes

Tempting taste treats will be twice as tantalizing when you display them
in dishes you make yourself.

Although any of the bowls and dishes shown in chapter 5 will do nicely,
perhaps you'd like to create something "fancier" for the living room.

This is easily done by cutting colored glass bottles and gluing the parts
into interesting shapes. For example, half-gallon wine jugs with rich green
tints can be cut into adorable basket-style candy dishes. Simply cut the bottom
of the jug about one or two inches high. Cut a ring from the same jug and

Stacked candy dishes are also handy for serving chips and dips.

Even plain glass bottles make elegant candy dishes with a bit of decoration. (Created by Arberta Lammers.)

fracture in half. Glue the half ring to the bottom and remove excess glue when dry. Fill with yummies!

Stacked candy dishes are just as easy. Select two matching colored jugs, one larger than the other. Use the top and bottom of the largest jug for the stem and first dish. Use the neck and bottom of the smaller jug for a second stem and dish. If desired, use another matching but smaller bottle for a third tier. Stacked candy dishes are not only handy to serve assorted candies, but they are excellent for serving chips and dips.

Clear glass bottles and jugs may also be transformed into eye-catching candy dishes with a bit of decoration. Any design may be applied using the same techniques learned in the preceding section for making mosaic candle holders. First, draw the design with a felt-tip pen; then follow the drawn lines with craft metal. Next, fill in the design with glass paints. If you want to waterproof the paint, use acrylic sealer (as explained under Bowls from Bottles, chapter 5).

Another clever idea for a candy dish is to glue flat marbles or glass globs (available in hobby stores) on the glass. Then circle the marbles with craft metal. You'll be amazed at the beautiful results!

Marbles and craft metal truly transform trash to treasure! (Created by Arberta Lammers.)

Remove excess glue and fill with yummies! (Created by Ila Mae Robinson.)

A basket-style candy dish is easily made with a green half-gallon jug and glue.

Domes

Keepsakes may be preserved forever in a dome of glass cut from a clear bottle. Select a bottle with as little writing in the glass as possible and cut at the desired height. To hang a keepsake from the dome, insert and glue a half ring. Affix the keepsake to the half ring and turn upside down. Use a bottle bottom or circle of wood for the base.

Whole bottles may also be used to preserve keepsakes. Simply cut the bottle at the bottom or top. Insert the keepsake—such as baby shoes, plastic flowers from candy boxes, or family heirlooms—and glue back together. This idea is also great for sealing ships in bottles!

Tongs may be needed to insert and glue a half ring to the inside of the dome.

Heirlooms are easily viewed yet well preserved in domes cut from bottles. (Created by Ila Mae Robinson.)

Cut bottle near top or bottom and fill with plastic flowers, ship, baby shoes, and so forth.

Glue bottle back together and display in living room.

Lampshades

The "play" of light behind colored or painted glass is so fascinating that lamps are a favorite creation of bottle artists.

First, find an electrified base to cover with a bottle art lampshade. Chances are that you may already have an old lamp in the attic that needs a new shade. If not, browse secondhand stores for lamp bases. Or, consult a salesman at the hardware or electrical supply store to see how easily you can make your own base.

Now, about the lampshade. The bottle or jug you select for the shade will, of course, depend upon the size of the base. Generally speaking, the larger the jug the better. Gallon jugs, for instance, are more easily decorated and usually fit far better than quart bottles. Select attractively shaped bottles; and, if you don't plan to decorate, use colored glass jugs. Cylinder-shaped lampshades may be made from two or three midsections cut from gallon jugs and glued together.

To decorate a lampshade, use any of the bottle art techniques discussed so far. Mosaic-style shades are particularly lovely when painted with bright crystallizing glass paints . . . light twinkles merrily through the crystallized patterns. Or, for an antique Tiffany-style lampshade, outline designs with craft metal and fill in with glass paints. For variety, use gold or silver craft metal and spray-paint the lamp base gold or silver to match.

Both mosaic and Tiffany lampshades can be decorated within an hour. If you prefer a longer-lasting project, try creating a lampshade from bottle bottoms!

The hanging lampshade pictured, for example, required sixty successfully cut matching green bottle bottoms. Use strong epoxy and glue one side at a time. When dry, glue on a frame of narrow glass strips cut freehand from green bottles. Finally, add molded plastic flowers to disperse light between the bottle bottoms. Such a lampshade is indeed a welcome luxury in any living room.

Find an old lamp base and select jugs or bottles that may be cut to fit.

Midsections cut from two one-gallon jugs become a lovely cylinder lampshade when decorated mosaic style. (Created by Ila Mae Robinson.)

Glass paints and craft metal enable bottle artists to re-create antique Tiffany lampshades. (Created by Ila Mae Robinson.)

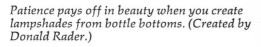

Patience pays off in beauty when you create lampshades from bottle bottoms. (Created by Donald Rader.)

Plaques

A bare living room wall can become the center of attention when you perk it up with bottle art plaques.

Plaques can be simple or ornate. For instance, simple plaques can be made from bottle bottoms hung with twine or colored yarn. Decorate the inside of the bottle bottom with decals, cutouts, photographs, seashells, agates, and such. Use heavy white craft glue to affix decorations to the glass.

Ornate plaques cut from bottle rings require more time and patience. But, as usual, your efforts will be rewarded with admiration. Cut whole rings, quarter rings, three-quarter rings—whatever size and shape you desire to complete the plaque. Use epoxy or silicone adhesive when gluing glass to glass. The centers of whole rings may be decorated with molded plastic designs, artificial flowers, beads, baubles, and so on. To make the gluing task easier, arrange your design on a counter or tabletop. Glue the center together first, working your way outward. You may wish to let the glue dry section by section rather than attempting to glue all at once.

Bottle rings can be the basis of a colorful, eye-catching wall plaque. (Created by Donald Rader.)

Simple plaques are easily made with bottle bottoms, cutouts, wide colored yarn, and glue.

Vases

Arranging flowers is a breeze if you're a bottle artist. Instead of arranging flowers to suit the vase, you can now cut a vase to suit the flowers!

Single roses or daffodils, for example, are nice displayed in tiny colored bottles. Chrysanthemums are lovely floating in brandy snifters cut from clear glass bottles. Medium-size flower arrangements fit well in stemmed vases cut from juice or cooking oil bottles. And fuller bouquets are beautiful displayed in vases made from half-gallon and gallon jugs.

The easiest vase is made with one cut. Select an interestingly shaped or nicely colored bottle in the size desired. Cut the bottle one inch from the bottom; invert the top; and glue the mouth to the bottom, which is now the base. Or, cut the bottle near the top; use the top as the base; and glue the bottle bottom to the neck.

If you have selected a clear glass bottle, it can be painted with glass paints in a color that blends with the flowers or living room decor.

Perhaps living room tables and shelves are already filled. No problem . . . just place your flowers in a hanging vase and suspend from the ceiling. Vases cut from bottles can easily be hung in nets made from raffia or macramé cord.

See what vases you can create with your new hobby!

Cut bottle one inch from bottom, invert top, and glue. (Created by Ila Mae Robinson.)

Glass paints that blend with flower or room colors enhance vases. (Created by Ila Mae Robinson.)

No room for vases? Hang them from the ceiling!
(Created by Ila Mae Robinson.)

Bottle tops can be cut into gracefully stemmed vases. (Created by Ila Mae Robinson.)

Chapter 8

Cut Bottles
for Every Room

Bottle creations are most often seen and admired in the kitchen, party room, and living room. But don't stop there! Bottle art can provide novel accessories for every room in the house.

Many of the projects you have already tried may be used in other rooms. For example, ashtrays are handy anywhere. Candle holders can shed soft lighting in bedrooms. Water glasses are dandy in bathrooms. And vases filled with fresh-cut or artificial flowers are cheerful in any room.

In addition, you can create special projects that fit in a particular room. Here are a few new ideas to tickle your imagination!

Bottles in the Bathroom

Just to prove that *any* room can be enhanced with bottle creations, let's start with the bathroom. Clear glass bottles can be cut and decorated in a matching set to hold cotton swabs, hairpins, lipsticks, and so on. Select four bottles—two beverage size and two half-gallon size—to make a bathroom glass, toothbrush holder, soap dish, and ashtray. Cut half-gallon jugs into stemmed mugs to hold bubble bath, dusting powder, or hair curlers.

In other words, you can conveniently display all your bathroom notions in containers cut from bottles!

You can even turn your bathroom into a "showplace" with bottle art. For example, an elegant soap dish can be made from a clear glass gallon jug. Cut the bottom of the jug an inch and a half high. Cut the top of the jug a few inches below the narrow neck. Turn the top upside down and glue to the bottom. Fill the bottom with artificial flowers; place guest soap in the top. Who would guess this creation was once an old jug?

Another "showplace" idea is to decorate a matching soap dish, water glass, and wastebasket. Cut a half-gallon jug up to two inches high for the soap dish. The water glass can be cut from a clear beer bottle or ketchup bottle. The wastebasket should be a gallon jug cut as tall as possible. Decorate with gold craft metal and crystallizing glass paints that blend with the bathroom's decor.

Bedroom Bottle Art

Naturally all ashtrays, vases, and candle holders in the bedroom are bottles decorated to match the room's motif! Why not go one step further and create lampshades that match the bedspreads or curtains? Just use glass paints or leftover fabric to decorate the lampshade cut from bottles.

An elegant soap dish begins with a clear gallon jug.

Add plastic flowers to the base and fill with guest soap. (Created by Ila Mae Robinson.)

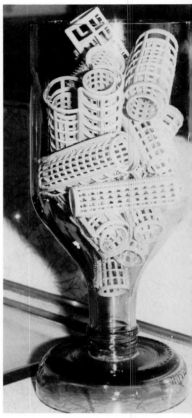

All bathroom notions can be conveniently displayed with bottle art. (Created by Ila Mae Robinson.)

Crystallizing glass paints turn ordinary bottles into an attractive soap dish, water glass, and wastebasket.

For example, an extremely clever lampshade can be made to match patchwork quilts. First, assemble materials: fabric cut into random shapes, craft glue, craft metal, electrical supplies, two one-gallon juice jugs, and epoxy. Cut the bottom from one gallon juice jug and the middle section from the second jug; use epoxy to glue together. Use craft glue to affix fabric piece by piece until the glass is completely covered.

After the glue has dried overnight, outline each different piece of fabric with craft metal. When the craft metal dries, the lampshade is ready to use.

If you wish to turn the lampshade into a hanging pendant lamp, simply run an electrical cord through a hole punched in the lid. Attach the cord to a socket. The socket may be held firmly in place with a threaded pipe, hex nut, and threaded brass ring. You may also braid the electrical cord through chain links if you want the lamp to hang from a chain. (Kits to electrify pendant lamps are available in hobby and hardware stores for about five dollars; but it's much cheaper to buy the parts separately and do it yourself.)

Another novel idea for the bedroom is a jewelry tree. There's no need to paw through drawers or cluttered boxes to find "those" earrings because they'll be readily available on a jewelry tree. Cut a pretty-colored green wine bottle near the neck; glue the remainder of the bottle to the neck. Cut rings and half rings from another green wine bottle and glue to the tree. Add as many rings as necessary to hold jewelry used most often. Clip earrings to whole rings; hang necklaces and bracelets from half rings.

Now, invent your own creation to hold jewelry or the contents of emptied pockets for the man of the house!

To make a patchwork lampshade, first glue fabric to a gallon juice jug.

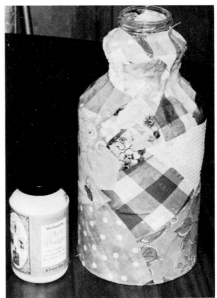

For a longer cylinder shape, add the middle of another jug and continue gluing fabric.

When glue has dried, outline each swatch with craft metal.

Make into a pendant lamp with receptacle, threaded pipe, hex nut, electrical cord, lid, and threaded brass ring.

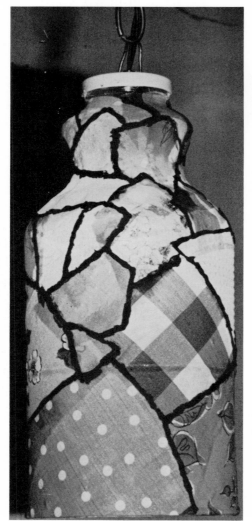

Lamps that match bedspreads or curtains are a welcome addition to the bedroom. (Created by Alberta Bainter.)

Jewelry trees are handy and attractive on bedroom dressers. (Created by Ila Mae Robinson.)

Dandies for the Den

Bottle art in the den or home office will be most appreciated if it's practical. Lamps, ashtrays, pencil holders, wastebaskets, are particularly useful. But do avoid fancy vases, ornate candle holders, and other items that serve no purpose and clutter up the working area.

Even with practical items, there's plenty of opportunity to be creative. For example, desk lamps are functional; but they're also attractive when made from beer bottle tops stacked about two feet high. Use an inverted ashtray for the base; electrify; and add a lampshade.

Dandy desk sets can also be made from bottle art. Cut a pencil holder from a beverage bottle. Make a wastebasket from two one-gallon jugs—using all but the neck of one jug and the midsection of the other. Glue together. Create an ashtray from the bottom of a gallon jug and two three-quarter rings cut from a beverage bottle. Glue the rings to the jug bottom. A cigarette can then burn safely in the resulting groove.

Decorate the desk set with decals, glass paints, or cover with contact paper.

Matching desk sets prove that projects for the den can be beautiful as well as practical. (Created by Ila Mae Robinson.)

Make a groove to hold a cigarette by gluing two three-quarter rings to the bottom of a gallon jug.

A useful and attractive desk lamp can be made from beer bottles. (Created by Yorkshire House, makers of the Miracle Bottle Cutter.)

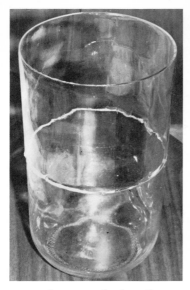

To make a wastebasket, first glue parts from two one-gallon jugs together.

Decorate with a pattern, decal, glass paints, or cover with contact paper. (Pattern from Glass Stain Patterns by Arberta, Number 70, published by the Titan Corporation.)

Handy Ideas for Hobby Rooms

Bottle art can be used to make containers for any other hobby. Clear glass beverage or ketchup bottles can be cut to hold hooks, swivels, blades, or what have you for the fisherman who makes his own lures. Clear glass canning jars are perfect holders for nails, screws, bits, and so forth in the shop of a do-it-yourself handyman. Artists can use small cut bottles to hold turpentine, brushes, and mediums. Seamstresses will enjoy the convenience of sewing notions readily available in cut bottle containers.

Generally speaking, you should not decorate or paint such containers. (They are useful because you can see through the glass.) Select bottles that are large enough for fingers or hands to reach into. And be sure to sand edges carefully so the user won't be cut.

Bottle art is also easily combined with other hobbies. Rock hounds can display polished agates in mugs or bowls cut from clear glass jugs. Woodworkers can create wooden lids or bases for their bottle art canisters and candle holders. Macramé enthusiasts can tie holders for hanging planters and fishbowls cut from bottles. Photographers can use bottle tops for funnels when mixing darkroom chemicals. See what you can create from bottles to complement your other hobbies!

Bottle art is easily combined with other hobbies such as sewing, fishing, macramé, carpentry. (Created by Ila Mae Robinson.)

Chapter 9

Bottle Art
Goes Outdoors

Outdoor accessories—such as wind chimes, patio lights, planters—are easily broken. By making and replacing these items with bottle art, you'll not only save many dollars, but you'll save needless worry. So what if a youngster throws a rock at your patio light? You can replace it in a jiffy!

Look around your yard to see what can be fashioned from cut bottles and jugs.

Greenhouse Accessories

The greenhouse is an excellent place to begin utilizing bottle art. One cut from a bottle cutting kit transforms any half-gallon or gallon jug into a perfect holder for starting plants. Or, try your hand at freehand cutting (see chapter 3) to provide unusually shaped planters for the greenhouse.

Jugs also make dandy lampshades in greenhouses. Simply remove the bottom from a jug and punch a hole in the lid for the electrical wires to come through. Such a lamp can provide heat for the plants and lighting for the gardener.

Practice freehand cutting on greenhouse planters . . . even mistakes can often be used! (Created by Donald Rader.)

Greenhouse lamps provide warmth as well as light. (Created by Donald Rader.)

Any gallon or half-gallon jug may be used for starting plants. (Created by Donald Rader.)

Patio Lights

Colorful patio lights can add festivity to outdoor parties and barbecues. If the light will be protected from the weather, you can make the light by using techniques already shown. If the light will not be protected, however, be sure to use electrical wiring made for outdoor use; waterproof glue; and acrylic sealer or spray varnish to protect decorations.

Small lights shaded with amber beer bottles are particularly popular outdoors, as are green wine bottles. Soft beverage bottles with "mod" lettering, such as 7-Up, also make charming patio lights. Or, add glitter or glass paint to clear bottles for more color. Still another idea is to glue bottles into interesting shapes.

Add glitter or glass paint to clear bottles for more colorful patio lights. (Created by Donald Rader.)

Try gluing bottle parts into interesting shapes. (Created by Donald Rader.)

Clear gallon jugs give Mother Nature a helping hand with fragile plants.

Plant Protectors

Give Mother Nature a helping hand with fragile plants by covering such plants with clear gallon jugs. Simply remove the bottom of the jug and place over the plant. This mini-greenhouse protects the plant from wind, animals, and inclement weather. Yet, the open neck allows moisture and fresh air to nourish the plant.

Pet Dishes

Dogs and cats will enjoy their own food and water bowls cut from matching bottles. Select gallon jugs for large animals and smaller bowls for cats and miniature dogs. Sand edges carefully. For a personalized touch, write the pet's name on the dishes with ball-point paint tubes.

Bottles and jugs may also be cut for use as bird feeders and for feeding small animals such as rabbits and chipmunks.

Your dog may insist on eating at the table when he has his own matched bowls!

Wind Chimes

You'll be amazed at the cheerful tinkling sound of wind chimes cut from bottles. And here's all you need to make a set: six bottle tops, string (leather thong or strong fish line), and the "pop-top" from six beverage cans.

Tie the string around the pop-top and insert through the first bottle neck. Tie another pop-top about two inches farther up the string and add the second bottle top. The pop-top holds the bottle in place so that each succeeding bottle will gently strike the underneath bottle when stirred by a breeze. (Each top serves as a "clapper" for the "bell" above.) Continue adding pop-tops and bottle tops to the string until it is as long as you desire. Various lengths and bottles will produce different tones.

Matching green or brown bottles make particularly attractive wind chimes. Or, alternate colors using brown-green-clear, brown-green-clear, and so on. Still another idea is to use all clear bottle tops and paint with glass paints. By painting the inside of the bottle top, you will not need to protect it further from rain and wear.

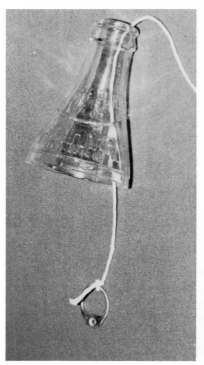

Start wind chimes from the bottom using pop-top, string, and bottle top.

Pop-tops hold bottles in place so that each bottle top serves as a "clapper" for the bottle above.

The length and weight of bottle tops will produce various tones. (Created by Ila Mae Robinson.)

Bottle art wind chimes are tinkly and cheerful. (Created by Ila Mae Robinson.)

If you are adept at cutting bottle rings, you'll find it fun to create wind chimes from rings rather than tops. Start from the top, using three small rings glued together or a large ring cut from a gallon jug for the centerpiece. Spread the rings on a tabletop and arrange at various distances from the centerpiece. Tie with string or fishline. When hung, the rings will sound like tinkling bells in a breeze. A stronger wind will transform this wind chime into a "whirling dervish," with rings dancing in exotic circles.

Spread rings on table and tie to centerpiece.

Wind chimes made from bottle rings not only tinkle . . . they dance too!

Chapter 10

Gifts from Bottles and Jugs

Thoughtful handmade gifts are always treasured most . . . especially when the gift is handmade bottle art. You cannot only create the perfect gift for every occasion, but you can personalize every gift by using favorite colors or names of friends and relatives. And, over the years, you can save hundreds of dollars by making rather than buying gifts.

Anniversary

Friends are sure to appreciate photographs framed in bottle rings to commemorate an anniversary. Use a series of photos taken throughout the years; pictures of their children; or photographs of the married couple. Cut rings from bottles that are slightly smaller than the pictures.

On the anniversary photo frame shown, for example, use 8" x 10" glossy photographs and rings two inches wide cut from a green gallon jug. Lay the ring on top of the photo exactly over the part you want framed. Draw a line around the circle and cut following this line. Cut the same size circle from a piece of stiff cardboard. Glue the photo and cardboard together.

Next, place the ring on its side and let it roll on a level table. When it stops rolling, the heaviest part of the bottle will be down. Glue the edge of the cardboard and insert in the frame, making sure the heavy part of the bottle is down. (Otherwise, the frame will roll around!) Let the glue dry overnight, and the gift will be ready for giving.

Anniversary photo frames can stand by themselves on a level surface, or they may be hung from the wall.

Happy couples are sure to appreciate anniversary photos framed in bottle rings.

Birthdays

If you frequently forget birthdays until the last minute, then you'll find a bottle cutting kit is really a lifesaver. In just a few minutes, you can create the perfect gift for man, woman, or child. Browse preceding chapters for quick and easy ideas.

If time is no problem, however, perhaps you'd like to try your hand at more elaborate gifts. Men friends, for example, will be pleased with a keepsake dome that contains an object they cherish. Select a bottle or jug of ample size to house the keepsake.

On the dome pictured, a clear glass gallon jug was cut as near the neck as possible. Next a wooden salad bowl and wooden drawer pull were stained walnut. A cup hook was screwed into the drawer pull and the pull glued to the dome. Another cup hook was glued to the side of the jug. Then the keepsake—in this case, grandfather's watch—was carefully hung inside. Finally, the dome was glued to the wooden base. The lucky recipient of a keepsake dome has a way to view and enjoy this heirloom.

When a woman friend has a birthday, thrill her with a neckscarf and earring set. First, select the neckscarf and try to find a colored bottle that matches. (Or, use clear glass rings and color with glass paints.) The neckscarf shown was red, white, and blue. So three rings were cut from a blue medicine bottle. The first ring, which was used on the scarf, only needs sanding. To make the second two rings into earrings, sand edges and glue on earring clips (available at hobby stores or use clips from old earrings). If "dangly" earrings are preferred, use thin gold or copper wire to attach to earring clip. More than likely, you'll be able to find old earrings in your jewelry box or at the secondhand store that will provide "parts" for bottle art earrings.

Now, for the kiddies. Their very favorite birthday presents will undoubtedly be fanciful animals you create from bottles. With various size beer bottles and a vivid imagination, you can make piggy banks, owls, birds, rabbits, and other items. Such animals, of course, require some freehand cutting (see chapter 3).

A careful inspection of the rabbit pictured will give you an inkling of the bottle parts that may be used to create animals. (Note that cotton was enclosed in two glued bottle bottoms for tail!) Use beads, pipe cleaners, and so on to add facial features.

When making animals, be sure to sand all edges carefully . . . wee ones will insist on touching these delightful creatures.

Coordinated neckscarf and earring sets will be used and admired by woman friends.

Floyd Fleming displays his clever creation, a cottontail rabbit, that is sure to delight youngsters. (Courtesy Fleming Bottle & Jug Cutters, Inc.)

Please men friends with keepsake domes containing objects they cherish. (Created by Ila Mae Robinson.)

Christmas

No holiday is more fun to decorate for than Christmas. And this year, decorating will be even more fun because you can use bottle art decorations for your own home as well as for gifts.

An easy Christmas project is candle holders. Cut bottles to fit various sizes of red, green, and/or gold candles. Place along a mantel, windowsill, or shelf. Between candle holders, place holly, pine cones, fir branches, Christmas figurines, or small wrapped packages.

Creations cut from bottles can also enhance holiday swags. For example, bells made from bottle tops add color and originality. Simply cut the top of a clear glass beverage or ketchup bottle and paint the inside with crystallizing glass paint. Use tiny Christmas balls, bells, or painted glass grape molds for a clapper. Attach to the bell with wire or pipestems. Two bells will be ample for small swags and look especially nice when wired onto the bow.

And, of course, no Christmas tree will be complete without ornaments made from bottles! Clever scene ornaments can easily be made with clear bottle bottoms and rings, craft metal, glass paints, craft glue, miniature figurines, and gold braid. Use craft metal first to add designs to bottle bottoms, sides, and/or edges. Then paint the outside of the glass with crystallizing or staining glass paints. Finally, glue miniature figurines, beads, plastic greenery, angel hair, and so forth to the glass.

Glue or tie gold braid around the ring to attach it to the branches. Your adorable handmade scene ornaments are now ready to add sparkle and interest to a Christmas tree.

Candle holders of all shapes and sizes may be spread across mantels, then decorated with evergreen branches and pine cones. (Created by Ila Mae Robinson.)

Holiday swags are enhanced by bells cut from bottles. (From Staining Glass, written by Arberta Lammers for the Titan Corporation.)

Glue tiny figurines, plastic greenery, and beads to glass with heavy white craft glue.

Decorate sides of rings with craft metal and glass paint.

Scene ornaments made from bottles add sparkle and interest to Christmas trees. (All scene ornaments created by Arberta Lammers.)

Housewarming

Most of the bottle creations pictured in earlier chapters would be appropriate housewarming gifts. Imagine, for example, how thrilled a family would be to receive an ornate candelabrum for the new living room . . . or a fancy soap dish for the bathroom . . . or lampshades made from wine bottles for the party room. You simply can't go wrong when you give bottle art!

A personalized touch is especially thoughtful on housewarming gifts. For instance, tumblers made from bottles are extra nice when you add the family's name or initial. Use waterproof gold craft paint from the hobby store.

It will be easy to add another personal touch if you know the colors used to decorate the home. You can then create vases, candy dishes, lampshades, candle holders, ashtrays, among other ideas, that exactly match your friend's color scheme.

No matter what you create for a housewarming gift, rest assured your handmade bottle art will be appreciated!

Add the family initial for a personal touch to housewarming gifts. (Created by Ila Mae Robinson.)

Decorate candle holders, vases, ashtrays, and so on in colors that match the new home's color scheme. (From Staining Glass, written by Arberta Lammers for the Titan Corporation.)

Baby's own toiletry set is easily made in less than half an hour.

New Baby

A nice way to say "Welcome to the World" is with baby's own toiletry set. Simply cut clear glass beer bottles four inches high, sand carefully, and affix appropriate decals. The matching set may then be filled with cotton balls, swabs, diaper pins, and so forth.

Ideas learned in other chapters also make nice baby gifts. For example, dainty decals could be applied to a matching dish set. Make a lampshade from a gallon jug and decorate with painted toys or animals. Or, make a dome of glass to preserve baby's first shoes.

Party Favors

Because bottle art is so inexpensive to make, you can easily create favors for party guests to keep. For cocktail parties, you could make cocktail glasses with each guest's name written on one with ball-point paint tubes. Small personalized glasses will also be a hit at children's birthday parties.

If the party is to celebrate a special occasion, such as wedding or anniversary, you could write the name of the couple and date of their marriage on mugs or ashtrays for guests to take home.

Nut cups make an especially nice favor for card parties. Cut four amber beer bottles about three inches high. Insert a card symbol (hearts, diamonds, spades, clubs) in each cup; affix with masking tape; and follow the pattern to paint the shape on the outside of the cup. No sanding will be necessary if you glue braid around the edge. Fill with nuts or mints. With your clever party favors, no cardplayer will go home a loser!

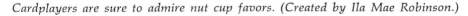

Cardplayers are sure to admire nut cup favors. (Created by Ila Mae Robinson.)

Insert a pattern inside the nut cup and paint the pattern on the outside.

Use heavy white glue to affix gold braid.

Wedding

Newlyweds will be grateful for any bottle art gift that you create. But they'll be especially pleased with a mug that displays their names and the date of the wedding.

To make a wedding mug, first find a nicely shaped half-gallon or gallon wine bottle. Clear glass is preferable. Cut and glue the bottle into a stemmed mug. Paint the outside of the mug with a crystallizing glass paint. Glue trim or braid to the edges of the mug and shape into a heart. When the glue has dried, write the couple's names and wedding date with a ball-point paint tube. Finally, spray carefully with acrylic sealer to protect the paint from wear.

Chapter 11

Professional
Bottle Art

Although most bottle artists begin the hobby as a pleasant pastime, it isn't long before the opportunity arises to make bottle cutting a profitable pastime also.

Friends see the clever cocktail glasses you have made, for example, and request a similar set. Perhaps you've made a wedding mug for a relative, and later that relative asks you to make another mug for a friend. Soon strangers are calling to say they have seen something you created and they would like to order a duplicate.

Professional bottle cutting begins as easily as that!

If you, too, would like to sell your bottle art, merely pass the word among friends and acquaintances. Put an ad in the classified section of the newspaper. Show your bottle creations to owners of gift shops, who will often be delighted to sell bottle art on a commission basis. Rent a booth at fairs or rummage sales. Contact tavern owners to see if they will sell creations from beer bottles as souvenirs. In no time, you'll have a nice income.

Remember always to sand edges carefully and use strong glue or epoxy so bottle art won't cut its buyer or fall apart. Happy customers are your best advertisers!

Now, what should you charge for bottle creations? First, add up the cost of materials used, such as glitter, glass paint, glue. Then determine how much per hour you wish to be paid, and keep track of time spent on each project. Name your price accordingly. For example, say you created a set of matching tumblers with decals. The bottles that you cut into tumblers were free, of course. But the decals cost about 50 cents. It took you about an hour to cut, sand, and affix the decals. And you want to make $5.00 an hour. The price for the set of tumblers would thus be $5.50.

Even if you don't choose to sell your bottle art, you'll still save hundreds of dollars by making your own dishes and household decorations and making gifts for friends.

Best yet, bottle art gives you hours of fun, a chance to express your creativity, and an interesting hobby that lasts a lifetime. And that makes the art of creative bottle cutting priceless!

Index